SCIENCE JOURNAL

McGRAW-HILL

SCIENCE

GRADE 3

LTX
1-200
Mcq
Grade 3
Journal

McGraw-Hill
School Division

New York   Farmington

W9-BIW-860

Table of Contents

Investigate Why Craters Are Different Sizes

Hypothesize Why are craters different sizes?

Write a **Hypothesis:** _____

_____

_____

How does the size of a falling marble affect the size of the crater it forms? How does the height of a falling marble affect its crater size?

Materials

- marbles of different sizes
- flour
- meterstick
- safety goggles
- aluminum pie tin
- newspaper
- ruler

Procedures

Safety Wear goggles.

1. **Make a Model** Place newspaper on a flat surface. Fill a pie tin with flour. Smooth the flour's surface.

2. **Observe** Compare the sizes of the marbles. Discuss with a partner which marble will make the biggest crater. What do you mean by big? Deep or wide, or both? Write your ideas.

_____

_____

3. **Measure** Drop the smallest marble into the flour from a height of 25 cm. Measure the size of the crater it creates. Record your results.

_____

4. **Measure** Repeat step 3 from heights of 50 cm, 75 cm, and 100 cm.

_____

5. **Repeat** Try the activity again with a large marble.

_____

Conclude and Apply

1. Interpret Data What happened to the size of the crater as the
marble was dropped from greater heights? Why?

_____

_____

2. Interpret Data What happened to the size of the crater as the
size of the marble increased? Why?

_____

_____

3. Infer Why are craters on the Moon different sizes?

_____

_____

 Inquiry

Think of your own questions that you might like to test using the flour and
aluminum pie tin. Why are craters on the Moon and Earth different shapes?

My Question Is:

_____

_____

How I Can Test It:

_____

_____

My Results Are:

_____

_____

Investigate the Features of Living Things

Hypothesize What features do you think living things have?
How could you test your ideas?

Write a **Hypothesis:**

_____

_____

Observe pea seeds and gravel to find out the features of living things.

Materials

- 25 pea seeds
- 25 pieces of gravel
- 1 hand lens
- 2 pieces of white paper
- 2 3½ oz. plastic cups
- water
- marker

Procedures

1. **Measure** Mark a piece of white paper A. Place the pea seeds on it. Mark another piece of paper B. Place the gravel on it.

2. **Observe** Look at the seeds and gravel with the hand lens. Describe what you see.

_____

_____

3. Mark a plastic cup A. Place the seeds in it. Mark the other plastic cup B. Place the gravel in it. Pour the same amount of water into each cup. Make sure the seeds and gravel are completely covered with water.

4. **Predict** What do you think will happen after two days?

_____

5. **Observe** Look at the soaked seeds and gravel every few hours for two days. Record your observations on another sheet of paper.

Conclude and Apply

1. **Explain** What happened to the seeds? What happened to the gravel? Which do you think is living? Why?

_____

_____

2. **Infer** What are some features of living things?

_____

_____

Going Further: Apply

3. **Compare and Contrast** From what you have observed, what are some differences between living and nonliving things?

_____

_____

Inquiry

Think of your own questions that you might test. How can you tell if other things are alive?

My Question Is:

_____

How I Can Test It:

_____

_____

My Results Are:

_____

Experimenting

How a Sow Bug Responds

If you lift up a large rock or log in a damp place you may find sow bugs. In this activity you will experiment to find out how a sow bug responds to changes in its environment.

Safety Wash hands after handling the sow bugs.

Materials

- 1 sow bug
- 1 hand lens
- ruler
- construction paper
- 1 toothpick

Procedures

1. **Observe** Place the sow bug on the paper. Take turns observing it with the hand lens. How does the sow bug move? Very gently, touch it with a toothpick. Record your observations.

_____

_____

2. **Plan** To test how the sow bug responds, plan several ways to change its environment. Be sure the changes will not harm the sow bug. Record your plans on the table below. Use if . . . then . . . statements that can be tested for each change.

If Statement	Then Statement	Results
If something gets in the sow bug's path	then it will change its path	
If . . .	then . . .	

3. Experiment Test the statement in the table. Record your results in the table.

4. Collect Data Test your own statements. Record the results in the table.

Conclude and Apply

Communicate Write a paragraph that describes how the sow bug responds to changes in its environment.

_____

_____

_____

_____

_____

Investigate What Organisms Need

Hypothesize What do you think organisms need to live and grow? How could you test your ideas?

Write a **Hypothesis:**

_____

_____

_____

_____

Observe caterpillars and pea plants to find out what organisms need to live and grow.

Materials

- container with 3 caterpillars and food
- soaked pea seeds from Topic 1
- 2 half-pint milk cartons
- 1½ cups soil
- hand lens
- water

Procedures

1. Plant 6 of the soaked pea seeds in each milk carton. Cover the seeds with ¾ cup of soil. Place one carton in a sunny area. Water it as needed. Place the other container in a dark place. Do not water it.

2. Place the container with the caterpillars in a cool place out of the sun.

3. **Observe** Look at the caterpillars and seeds two or three times each week. Record what you see.

_____

_____

_____

_____

Conclude and Apply

1. **Explain** What happened to the caterpillars?

_____

_____

2. **Draw Conclusions** What do caterpillars need to live and grow?
What do pea plants need to grow?

_____

_____

3. **Infer** What do pea plants get from the soil?

_____

Going Further: Apply

4. **Draw Conclusions** How are the needs of caterpillars different
from those of pea plants?

_____

_____

Inquiry

Think of your own questions that you might test. Do all plants need
soil, water, and sunlight to thrive?

My Question Is:

_____

How I Can Test It:

_____

My Results Are:

_____

Watch Water Travel Through a Plant!

Hypothesize How does water travel through a plant?

Write a **Hypothesis:**

_____

_____

_____

Materials

- 1 clear plastic container
- food coloring
- safety goggles

- 1 celery stalk with leaves
- water

Procedures

Safety Wear goggles.

1. **Measure** Put about 2 inches (5 cm) of water in the plastic glass. Add 10 drops of food coloring.

2. **Predict** Put a celery stalk in the glass for 2 hours. What do you think will happen?

_____

_____

Conclude and Apply

1. **Explain** What did you observe after 2 hours?

_____

_____

2. **Infer** How does water travel through a plant?

_____

_____

Going Further Stems contain numerous tube-like structures running from the roots to the leaves. How can you demonstrate that water travels in separate "tubes" in a stem? Write and conduct an experiment.

My Hypothesis Is:

_____

_____

My Experiment Is:

_____

_____

_____

_____

_____

_____

My Results Are:

_____

_____

Investigate How an Organism Changes as It Grows

Hypothesize How does a caterpillar change over its lifetime? How could you find out?

Write a **Hypothesis:**

_____

_____

Observe and record how a caterpillar grows and develops over a period of time.

Materials

• caterpillars and container from Topic 2   • 1 hand lens

Procedures

1. **Observe** Look at the caterpillars with the hand lens. Make a drawing of them.

2. **Observe** Look at the caterpillars twice each week. Record your findings and make a drawing of what they look like on a separate piece of paper. Answer these questions: How have the animals changed? How do the animals act?

_____

_____

_____

_____

Conclude and Apply

1. Explain What happened to the caterpillars?

_____

_____

2. Explain What does the caterpillar become when it is an adult?

_____

3. Compare In what ways are the young and adult forms different?

_____

_____

_____

Going Further: Apply

4. Classify How many different forms of development do the caterpillars go through?

_____

Inquiry

Think of your own questions that you might test. Do all animals go through the same stages of development?

My Question Is:

_____

_____

How I Can Test It:

_____

My Results Are:

Name that Trait Game!

Hypothesize What traits do you think you inherited from your parents? What things did you learn? Make a list for each.

Write a **Hypothesis:**

_____

_____

_____

Materials

• 8 index cards

Procedures

1. Write a trait that can be inherited on each of two cards. Write a trait that can be learned on each of the other two cards. Do not show your partner what you write.

2. Take turns holding up a card. Ask your partner to identify the trait as inherited or learned.

Conclude and Apply

1. **Classify** Arrange the cards into two groups.

2. **Communicate** Make an illustrated chart of the traits. Evaluate your results. Use a separate piece of paper if you need more room.

Inherited Traits	Learned Traits

Going Further What talents run in your family? Do your parents, grandparents, aunts, uncles, and cousins have the same careers or hobbies? List the jobs or hobbies that are common in your family. Discuss if the similarities indicate inherited or learned traits and make a table of family traits.

My Hypothesis Is:

_____

_____

My Experiment Is:

_____

_____

_____

_____

_____

My Results Are:

_____

_____

_____

Investigate How a Plant Life Cycle Begins

Hypothesize How does a plant's life begin? How could you test your ideas?

Write a **Hypothesis:**

_____

_____

Grow a pea plant to observe the beginnings of its life cycle.

Materials

- 5 pea seeds
- 1 plastic cup
- 1 self-sealing plastic bag, pint-sized
- ¼ cup of water
- 1 hand lens
- paper towel

Procedures

1. **Observe** Look at the seeds with a hand lens. Record your observations.

   _____

   _____

2. Soak the seeds in water in the cup overnight. Make sure the seeds are totally covered with water.

3. **Observe** Look at the seeds the next day. How are they different? Peel away the outside of one seed. Look at the seed with a hand lens. Record your observations. Separate the two halves of the seed. Use a hand lens to observe each half. Draw what you see on a separate piece of paper.

   _____

   _____

4. Moisten a paper towel. Fold it and place it inside the plastic bag. Place the other four seeds at the bottom of the plastic bag on top of the paper towel. Seal the bag.

5. Predict How do you think the peas will change? Observe the peas each day. Make drawings on a separate piece of paper to show how the peas change.

_____

Conclude and Apply

1. Explain How did the seeds change after they were soaked? What did you find between the two halves of the seed?

_____

_____

2. Infer Which part of the plant's life cycle is the seed?

_____

Going Further: Apply

3. Explain What changes did you observe as the tiny plants grew from the seeds?

_____

 **Inquiry**

Think of your own questions that you might test. Do all plants follow the same stages of development?

My Question Is:

_____

_____

How I Can Test It:

_____

My Results Are:

_____

Light or Shade

Hypothesize Do seedlings need light to grow?

Write a **Hypothesis:**

_____

Materials

- 2 pea seedlings from the Explore Activity
- 2 10-ounce clear plastic glasses
- water
- 2 paper towels
- 1 sheet of black construction paper
- tape
- scissors

Procedures

1. Cover the outside of one glass with black paper.

2. Wet the paper towels. Place one in each plastic glass. Put a seedling on the paper towel in each glass.

3. Place both glasses on a sunny window sill. Place a piece of the black paper over the top of the covered glass. Make sure the towels are kept wet.

4. **Observe** Compare the seedlings after two days.

Conclude and Apply

1. **Observe** What happened to the seedlings in the glass covered with the black paper? What happened to the other seedling?

_____

_____

2. Infer What does this tell you about a seedling's needs?

_____

_____

Going Further Do plants need sunlight or will plants thrive in artificial light? Write a hypothesis and design an experiment.

My Hypothesis Is:

_____

_____

_____

My Experiment Is:

_____

_____

_____

My Results Are:

_____

_____

Design Your Own Experiment

What Are the Parts of an Insect and a Plant?

Hypothesize What is the job of an organism's outer covering?
How could you test this idea?

Write a **Hypothesis:**

_____

_____

_____

Materials

- caterpillars in a 5-inch clear plastic petri dish
- 1 sheet of white paper
- 1 pea plant from Topic 2 Explore Activity
- 1 hand lens
- 1 toothpick
- paper towels

Procedures

1. **Observe** Look at the caterpillars with a hand lens. What parts do
   you see? Draw a caterpillar on a separate piece of paper.

   _____

   _____

2. **Experiment** Use the materials to observe how a caterpillar uses
   certain parts of its body. How does it move?

   _____

   _____

3. **Observe** Think of ways to closely examine the pea plant. Draw
   the parts of the plant on a separate piece of paper.

   _____

   _____

Conclude and Apply

1. **Explain** What are the parts of a caterpillar? How does a caterpillar use it parts?

_____

_____

_____

2. **Explain** What are the parts of a pea plant?

_____

Going Further: Apply

3. **Infer** How do you think the pea plant uses its parts?

_____

_____

_____

Inquiry

Think of your own questions that you might test. What are the parts of other organisms? Do all plants have the same parts?

My Question Is:

_____

_____

How I Can Test It:

_____

My Results Are:

_____

Classifying

Comparing Different Body Parts

Classifying information helps you make sense out of the world. How could you classify the parts of different organisms?

Procedures

1. List at least ten different plants and animals.

_____

_____

2. **Communicate** The table below shows headings for the types of parts you learned about in this topic.

Organisms With Similar Parts	
Parts That Protect and Support	
Moving Parts	
Parts That Take in Materials	
Parts That Get Information	

3. **Classify** In the table, group together organisms from your list that have similar parts.

Conclude and Apply

1. Identify Which organisms have similar parts that protect and support? Which organisms have similar moving parts?

_____

_____

_____

_____

_____

_____

_____

2. Identify Which organisms have similar parts that take in materials? Which organisms have similar parts that get information?

_____

_____

_____

_____

3. Classify Look at your list of plants and animals. How else might you group these organisms? Make a new table on another sheet of paper that shows another way to classify them.

Investigate the Smaller Parts of Living Things

Hypothesize How could you get a better look at some of the smaller parts of living things?

Write a **Hypothesis:**

_____

_____

_____

Observe the smaller parts of a pea plant and caterpillar.

Materials

- 1 pea plant from Topic 5
- 1 caterpillar in a petri dish
- 1 hand lens
- textbook

Procedures

1. **Observe** Look at the leaf of the pea plant very closely with the hand lens. Look at the caterpillar very closely with the hand lens. Describe what you see.

_____

_____

_____

2. **Observe** Now look at the pictures on page 55 of your textbook. They show the smaller parts of a caterpillar and a pea plant very close up.

3. Infer Which picture belongs to the caterpillar? Pea plant? Why do you think so?

_____

_____

Conclude and Apply

1. Explain What clues helped you identify which organism the pictures belonged to?

_____

Going Further: Apply

2. Infer What would you need to see the smaller parts of an organism?

_____

 **Inquiry**

Think of your own questions that you might test. Do the smaller parts of all plants and animals look the same?

My Question Is:

_____

_____

How I Can Test It:

_____

_____

My Results Are:

_____

_____

Get to Know the Back of Your Hand

Hypothesize How small is a cell?

Write a **Hypothesis:**

_____

Materials

• pen
• beans

Procedures

1. **Predict** With the pen, make the smallest dot you can on the back of your hand. How many cells do you think it covers? Write your prediction.

_____

2. **Use Numbers** Place all the beans in a solid circle. How many beans do you have?

_____

Conclude and Apply

Drawing Conclusions Each bean represents a skin cell under the dot on your hand. How many skin cells are under the ink dot? How does your prediction compare to this number?

_____

_____

Going Further Are different types of cells the same size and shape?
Design and conduct an experiment to find out.

My Hypothesis Is:

_____

_____

My Experiment Is:

_____

_____

_____

_____

My Results Are:

_____

_____

Investigate How Things Move

Hypothesize How much faster do you run than walk? How might you test your ideas?

Write a **Hypothesis:**

_____

Compare the time it takes you to run a certain distance with the time it takes you to walk that same distance.

Materials

- stopwatch
- 1 blue crayon
- 1 red crayon
- meter tape
- graph paper

Procedures

1. **Predict** Look at a distance of 10 meters. How long will it take you to run 10 meters? How long will it take you to walk 10 meters? Record your predictions.

   _____

   _____

2. **Measure** Use the stopwatch to time how long it takes each person in your group to run 10 meters. Record each person's time on a separate sheet of paper.

3. **Measure** Time how long it takes each person in your group to walk 10 meters. Record each person's time on a separate sheet of paper.

Conclude and Apply

1. **Compare** Look at your predictions of how long it would take you to walk and run 10 meters. How do they compare to the times you measured?

   _____

2. Communicate Print each person's name on the line at the bottom of the graph paper. Print the time in seconds on the left side of the graph. Use a red crayon to mark an X above your name to show how many seconds it took to walk 10 meters. Use a blue crayon to mark an X that shows how many seconds it took to run 10 meters.

3. Interpret Data What is the difference, in seconds, between your times for walking and running?

_____

Going Further: Problem Solving

4. Predict Use your graph to predict how long it would take you to walk 20 meters.

_____

_____

Inquiry

Think of your own questions that you might like to test. How does the slope of the ground affect how fast you walk?

My Question Is:

_____

How I Can Test It:

_____

_____

My Results Are:

_____

Picture the Position

Hypothesize Do position words help you give directions?

Write your **Hypothesis:**

_____

_____

Materials

• 2 sets of 5–7 blocks
• a notebook

Procedures

1. Sit opposite your partner at a table. Prop up the notebook between you. Create a building with your blocks.

2. **Communicate** By describing the position of each of your blocks, instruct your partner to create the same building.

3. **Compare** Remove the notebook. Are the buildings the same? Switch roles and try it again.

Conclude and Apply

Draw Conclusions What would happen if your partner gave you directions without using position words? Could you still build the building?

_____

_____

_____

_____

_____

Going Further Pick an object in the room. Without naming the object, write down directions on a separate piece of paper to tell your partner how to find the object. Describe your object's position by comparing it to the positions of other objects. Was your partner able to find the object you were describing?

Investigate Why Some Objects
Are Harder to Pull

Hypothesize Why are some objects harder to push or pull than others? How might you test your ideas?

Write a **Hypothesis:**

_____

_____

Measure the strength of different pulls.

Materials

• spring scale   • safety goggles   • 5 objects from your classroom

Procedures

Safety Wear goggles.

1. **Observe** Look at your spring scale. What is the highest your

   scale can read? _____

2. **Predict** Which one of the objects will require the greatest pull to move? Record your prediction. Then predict which object will require the next strongest pull to move. Record this prediction. Make a prediction for each of your objects.

   _____

   _____

3. **Measure** Hook the scale on an object. Place the scale and the object on a smooth, flat surface and pull at a steady speed. Record what the spring scale reads. Repeat with other classroom objects. Were your predictions correct?

   _____

   _____

Conclude and Apply

1. **Identify** What did you feel when you pulled an object on the spring scale?

_____

2. **Identify** Which objects made the scale read the highest when you pulled them?

_____

3. **Explain** Why did it take a bigger pull to move some objects?

_____

Going Further: Apply

4. **Experiment** How could you measure the strength of the pull needed to move your lunch box? If you took your lunch out of your lunch box, how would that affect your measurement?

_____

_____

Inquiry

Think of your own questions that you might like to test. How can you predict which of two objects requires more strength to lift?

My Question Is:

_____

How I Can Test It:

_____

My Results Are:

_____

Interpreting Data

Reading a Bar Graph

The bar graph below shows how much the dog weighs on each planet and on the Moon. Each bar gives us information, or *data*. For example, look at the bar labeled Earth. It lines up with 40 on the Pounds scale on the left. Now look at the bar labeled Jupiter. What number on the Pounds scale does it line up with? By answering this question, you are interpreting data.

Interpret the data in this graph to answer the questions below.

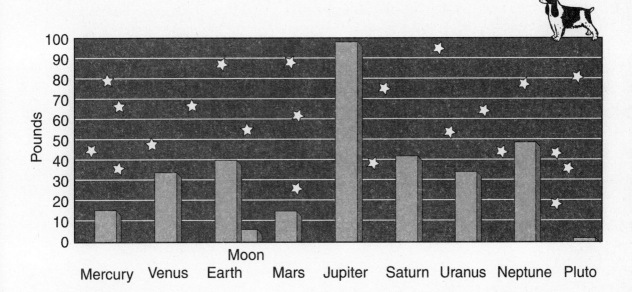

Procedures

1. **Interpret Data** How much does the dog weigh on Mars?

_____

2. **Interpret Data** On which planets would the dog weigh more than on Earth? On which planets would the dog weigh less?

_____

_____

_____

3. Compare How much heavier is the dog on Jupiter than
on Venus?

_____

_____

Conclude and Apply

Communicate Make a chart showing how you interpreted the data
from the graph in question 2.

Investigate What Causes a Change in Motion

Hypothesize Sometimes objects change position, and sometimes they stay still. What must you do to make a resting object move? How might you test your ideas?

Write a **Hypothesis:**

_____

_____

Experiment to find out what makes a resting object move.

Materials
- scissors
- washers
- string
- 2 paper clips
- safety goggles

Procedures **Safety** Wear goggles.

1. Cut two pieces of string that are slightly shorter than the width of your desk. Knot the strings together. Lay the knot in the middle of your desk and let the strings hang off opposite sides of the desk. Bend the paper clips to make hooks, and tie one to the free end of each string.

2. **Predict** Hold the knot in place and hang two washers on one paper-clip hook. What will happen if you let go of the knot? Write your prediction. Test your prediction.

_____

3. **Predict** Take the two washers off. Holding the knot in place, add one washer to each of the paper-clip hooks. Predict what will happen if you let go of the knot now. Test your prediction.

_____

4. **Experiment** What could you do with the washers to move the knot toward one side of the desk? Test your idea.

_____

Conclude and Apply

1. Compare What did you observe in steps 2 and 3?

_____

_____

2. Explain In step 3, why didn't the knot move? In step 4, what did you do to make the knot move?

_____

_____

Going Further: Problem Solving

3. Experiment How could you move the knot back to the middle of your desk?

_____

 Inquiry

Think of your own questions that you might like to test.
Does changing the length of the string make a difference?

My Question Is:

_____

_____

How I Can Test It:

_____

_____

My Results Are:

_____

_____

_____

Marbles in Motion

Hypothesize How can marbles help you reduce friction?

Write a **Hypothesis:**

_____

_____

Materials

- 10–20 marbles
- jar lid
- wooden block

Procedures

1. **Observe** Push the wooden block over the surface of your desk. Describe how it feels.

_____

2. **Experiment** Place the marbles under the jar lid. Lay the block on top of the lid.

3. **Observe** Push the block over the surface of your desk again. How does it feel now?

_____

Conclude and Apply

1. **Identify** When did you feel more friction: When you pushed the block by itself or over the jar lid?

_____

2. **Explain** How did the marbles help to reduce friction?

_____

_____

Going Further What would happen if you placed a piece of sandpaper under the block and tried to push it across your desk?

_____

_____

_____

Investigate What Work Is

Hypothesize What do you think work is? In your own words, write a definition of work. How might you apply your definition of work to different kinds of actions?

Write a **Hypothesis:**

_____

_____

Use your definition of work to classify the actions below. Does your definition of work make sense?

Materials

• 4 books   • pencil

Procedures

1. **Experiment** Complete each of the actions described below.
   • Put four books on the floor. Lift one book up.
   • Put four books on the floor. Lift all four up.
   • Put a book on your desk. Push down very hard on top of the book.
   • Pick up a pencil from your desk.
   • Push against a wall with all of your strength.

2. **Classify** After each action, ask yourself: "Did I do work?" Review the definition of work that you wrote. Does the action you did fit your definition? Tell your partner what you think. Together, decide whether the action was work or not.

_____

_____

_____

_____

_____

Conclude and Apply

1. **Evaluate** Look at your responses to the question "Did I do work?" Think about your responses. Is there a pattern? What is it?

_____

_____

2. **Communicate** On a separate piece of paper, write a sentence for each action explaining why you classified it the way you did.

Going Further: Apply

3. **Evaluate** How might different people classify the actions? For example, would picking up one book be work for a baby? Would picking up four books be work for a very strong adult?

_____

_____

_____

_____

Inquiry

Think of your own questions that you might like to test. Is homework work?

My Question Is:

_____

How I Can Test It:

_____

My Results Are:

_____

Changing Energy

Hypothesize What will happen when you rub a wooden block with sandpaper?

Write a **Hypothesis:**

_____

_____

_____

Materials

- wooden block
- sandpaper

Procedures

1. **Observe** Feel the temperature of the block.

2. **Observe** Rub the block with sandpaper about 20 times. What do you feel through your fingertips?

_____

_____

Conclude and Apply

Explain What happened to the temperature of the block?

_____

_____

Going Further You've stayed outside for too long building a snow fort. Your feet are freezing. How might you use friction to warm up your feet?

_____

_____

_____

Design Your Own Experiment

How Can You Make Work Easier?

Hypothesize Sometimes you want to move an object that takes a lot of force to move. How can you do it? How might you test your ideas?

Write a **Hypothesis:**

_____

_____

Materials

• a roll of masking tape   • safety goggles   • building materials

How Can You Make Work Easier?
Procedures

 Safety Wear goggles.

1. **Ask Questions** How can you invent a way to get the roll of tape from the floor to your desk? Your hands can help provide the lift, but you can't just pick up the tape and put it on the desk.

2. **Communicate** With your group members, think of as many different ways as you can to lift the tape. Write or draw two of your plans below. Use another sheet of paper if necessary.

3. **Experiment** After your teacher approves your plans, try one of them. Write down what happens. Does the plan work well? If not, what can you do to fix it? Try your other plan for lifting the tape.

_____

_____

_____

Conclude and Apply

1. Compare and Contrast Which of your two plans worked better?

_____

_____

2. Identify What materials did you use in your most successful invention?

_____

_____

3. Explain What forces did you use? What force did you work against?

_____

_____

Going Further: Apply

4. Evaluate Why did you think some plans for lifting the tape worked better than others?

_____

_____

 Inquiry

Think of your own questions that you might like to test. If you had different materials, would you have been able to lift the tape?

My Question Is:

_____

How I Can Test It:

_____

My Results Are:

_____

Make a Lever

Hypothesize What happens when you change the position of the fulcrum on a lever?

Write a **Hypothesis:**

_____

_____

_____

Materials

- clay
- ruler
- pencil
- 2 small blocks

Procedures

1. Use some clay to hold a pencil in place on your desk. Place the ruler over the center of the pencil.

2. **Experiment** Put 2 blocks on one end of your ruler. Add pieces of clay to the other end of the ruler. How much clay does it take to lift the blocks? What happens if you take a block away?

_____

_____

_____

3. **Experiment** Change the position of the ruler on the pencil. Then repeat step 2. How does the new position change your results?

_____

_____

_____

_____

Conclude and Apply

1. **Communicate** Draw your lever in the space below. Label the force, load, and fulcrum. Describe how your lever works.

_____

_____

_____

2. **Draw Conclusions** How does the position of the pencil affect the amount of force you need to lift the load?

_____

_____

_____

Going Further Name some levers that you have seen in action.

_____

_____

_____

Investigate How a Ramp Can Make Work Easier

Hypothesize When people built pyramids many years ago, they may have used a ramp to help them move rocks. How can a ramp make work easier? How might you test your ideas?

Write a **Hypothesis:**

_____

_____

Evaluate how a ramp can make work easier.

Materials

- 1 meter wooden board
- thin spiral notebook
- safety goggles
- spring scale
- 30 cm piece of string
- chair
- meter stick

Procedures   **Safety** Wear goggles.

1. Lean one end of the wooden board on the chair. Tie one end of the string around the bottom of the spring scale and the other end to the middle of the spiral wire of the notebook.

2. **Measure** Measure the pull needed to lift the notebook straight up to the height of the chair's seat. Then measure the distance you pulled the book. Record your measurements.

_____

_____

3. **Measure** Measure the pull needed to move the notebook up the board to the seat of the chair. Then measure the distance you pulled the book. Record your measurements.

_____

_____

4. Experiment Adjust the board so it is at a steeper angle.
Repeat step 3.

_____

_____

Conclude and Apply

1. Interpret Data Look at your measurements. Which method of
moving the notebook required more force? Which method
required moving the notebook a greater distance?

_____

_____

2. Compare Think about the three methods. What is the advantage
of each one? What is the disadvantage?

_____

_____

_____

_____

Going Further: Apply

3. Evaluate Which method would you use to put a stuffed animal onto
a shelf? Which method would you use to put a bike into a truck?

_____

_____

? Inquiry

Think of your own questions that you might like to test. What effect does the pulling surface have on the force required?

My Question Is:

_____

_____

How I Can Test It:

_____

_____

My Results Are:

_____

_____

Using Numbers

Evaluating Differences

You know that a screw is a simple machine that makes work easier. A screw makes work easier just like any other inclined plane—by letting you use less force over a greater distance. Screws come in many shapes and sizes. Some screws make work easier than others. How can one screw make work easier than another?

The diagram below shows three screws. In this activity you will use numbers to evaluate how each screw is different. Then you will use that information to infer which screw makes work the easiest.

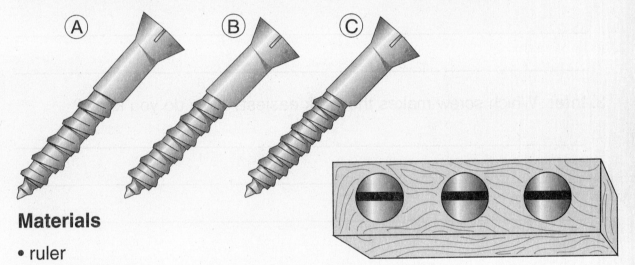

Materials

• ruler

Procedures

1. **Measure** What is the width of the head of each screw? What is the length of each screw? Record your measurements in the table.

2. **Use Numbers** What is the number of threads on each screw? Record the information in the table.

Screw	A	B	C
Head width			
Length			
Number of threads			

Conclude and Apply

1. **Compare** How does the width and length of each screw compare? How does the number of threads on each screw compare?

   _____

   _____

   _____

2. **Explain** How does the number of threads on each screw relate to the length of its inclined plane?

   _____

   _____

3. **Infer** Which screw makes the work easiest? How do you know?

   _____

   _____

   _____

Investigate Which Object Takes Up More Space

Hypothesize What will happen when you put different objects in a container of water? How might you test your ideas?

Write a **Hypothesis:**

_____

_____

Test which object takes up more space by placing different objects in a container of water.

Materials

- 12-oz. plastic cup half full of water
- markers (different colors)
- a piece of clay
- classroom objects

Procedures

1. **Measure** Find the level of the water. Use a marker to mark the level on the outside of the cup.

2. **Predict** What will happen to the level of the water when you place the piece of clay in the cup? Record your prediction.

_____

3. **Observe** Place the clay in the cup. What happens? Use a different color marker to mark the new water level on the outside of the cup. Remove the clay.

_____

4. **Predict** Look at the other objects. Which object will make the water level change the most when you put it in the cup? Record your prediction.

_____

5. **Experiment** Place one object at a time in the cup. Mark the new water level for each object. Use a different color marker for each object.

Conclude and Apply

1. **Identify** What happened each time you placed an object in the cup? Why?

_____

_____

2. **Compare and Contrast** How did the different objects affect the water level? Why do you think this happened?

_____

_____

3. **Draw Conclusions** Which object takes up the most space? How do you know?

_____

_____

Going Further: Problem Solving

4. **Experiment** What do you think will happen to the water level in the cup if you change the shape of the clay?

_____

_____

 Inquiry

Think of your own questions that you might like to test. Will a heavy object or a light object cause a greater change in the water level? Write your question, a way to test your question, and your results on a separate sheet of paper.

Measuring Mass

Hypothesize Do objects in your classroom have different masses?

Write a **Hypothesis:**

_____

_____

Materials

• balance   • small objects   • 30 paper clips

Procedures

1. Estimate the mass of each object. Record your estimates.

_____

_____

2. **Measure** Measure the mass of each object. Place the object on one side of the balance. Place paper clips on the other side until the two sides balance. Record the number of paper clips used to balance each object in the table below.

3. **Use Numbers** What is the mass of each object?
   (Remember, two paper clips equals about one gram.)
   Record the mass of each object in the table.

Object	Number of Paper Clips	Mass of Object

Conclude and Apply

1. **Compare and Contrast** How does your list of estimated masses compare with the measurements you recorded?

_____

2. **Plan** If you wanted to find the mass of your shoe, how could you do it? How many paper clips would you need?

_____

_____

Going Further A nickel equals about 5 grams. How can you use nickels to find the mass of objects in your classroom? Write and conduct an experiment.

My Hypothesis Is:

_____

_____

_____

My Experiment Is:

_____

_____

_____

My Results Are:

_____

_____

_____

Design Your Own Experiment

How Can You Classify Matter?

Hypothesize How can you tell whether a material is a solid or a liquid? How might you test your ideas?

Write a **Hypothesis:**

_____

_____

_____

Materials

- investigation tools
- plastic container of Oobleck
- newspaper
- safety goggles

Procedures   **Safety** Wear goggles.

1. **Observe** Observe the Oobleck using only your senses. How does the Oobleck look? What does it feel like? Record all of your observations.

_____

_____

2. **Experiment** Using the tools given to you, investigate the Oobleck in different ways. What new things do you observe? Record these observations.

_____

_____

3. **Classify** Look at the observations of Oobleck that you have made. Then review the definitions of solid and liquid that you wrote. Do you think Oobleck is a solid or a liquid? Could it be both? Why?

_____

_____

Conclude and Apply

1. **Communicate** What observations did you make about the properties of Oobleck?

   _____

   _____

2. **Explain** How did you decide to classify Oobleck? What observations helped you make your decision?

   _____

   _____

Going Further: Problem Solving

3. **Hypothesize** What do you think Oobleck is made of? How might you find out whether your idea is correct?

   _____

   _____

? Inquiry

Think of your own questions that you might like to test. What else can you find out about Oobleck?

My Question Is:

_____

How I Can Test It:

_____

My Results Are:

_____

_____

Communicating

Making a Table

When you communicate you share information with others. Scientists communicate what they learn from an experiment. They might tell people how they think new information can be used. You can communicate by talking, or by creating a drawing, chart, table, or graph.

You can communicate what you know about the properties of solids, liquids, and gases. Look at the drawing on this page to help you answer the questions below.

Procedures

1. **Observe** Look at the drawing. What forms of matter do you see? What properties do these forms have? Record your observations.

_____

_____

_____

_____

_____

2. Communicate Use your observations to fill in the table.

Forms of Matter	Properties

Conclude and Apply

1. Draw Conclusions What do solids and liquids have
in common? What makes them different?

_____

_____

_____

2. Communicate Give an example of a solid, a liquid, and a gas.
Then write a sentence that tells what you know about the shape
and volume of each one.

_____

_____

_____

_____

Investigate What Magnets Attract

Hypothesize What kinds of items will be attracted to a magnet?

Write a **Hypothesis:**

_____

_____

Materials

- magnet
- several objects

Procedures

1. **Observe** Look at your objects. What properties of the objects do you observe? Record your observations.

   _____

2. **Predict** Which of the objects will be attracted to a magnet?

   Record your predictions. _____

   _____

3. **Experiment** Test your predictions. Get a magnet from your teacher. Test each object to see if it is attracted to the magnet. Record the result of each test.

   _____

   _____

Conclude and Apply

1. **Classify** Look at the results of your tests. Which objects were attracted to the magnet? Which objects were not? Make two lists on a separate sheet of paper. In one list, write the names of the objects attracted to the magnet. In the other list, write those that were not. Title each of the lists.

2. Compare and Contrast Read the list of objects that were attracted to the magnet. Can you identify any properties that they all have in common? Write down your thoughts. Now look at the list of objects that were not attracted to the magnet. What kinds of things can you say about these objects? Write down your thoughts.

_____

_____

Going Further: Apply

3. What conclusions can you draw about the kinds of things that are attracted to magnets?

_____

_____

_____

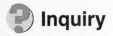 **Inquiry**

Think of your own questions that you might like to test. Can a magnet be used to separate objects?

My Question Is:

_____

How I Can Test It:

_____

_____

My Results Are:

_____

Bowl of Iron

Hypothesize If you read the label on a box of breakfast cereal, you'll probably see iron in the list of ingredients. Does breakfast cereal really contain iron?

Write a **Hypothesis:**

_____

_____

Materials

- 1 package fortified cereal
- plastic sandwich bag
- magnet
- sheet of white paper

Procedures

1. Pour the cereal into a plastic bag. Add the magnet and seal the bag.

2. Shake the bag for several minutes. Carefully remove the magnet. Hold it over a sheet of white paper.

3. **Observe** What do you see when you look at the magnet?

_____

_____

Conclude and Apply

Predict What would happen if you tried the same experiment using cereal that did not contain iron?

_____

_____

Going Further Do different breakfast cereals contain different amounts of iron? How can you compare the amount of iron in different cereals? Write and conduct an experiment.

My Hypothesis Is:

_____

_____

_____

My Experiment Is:

_____

_____

_____

_____

My Results Are:

_____

_____

_____

_____

Investigate How Heat Affects Different Materials

Hypothesize You could measure how hot soil and water get when they are exposed to the same amount of heat. Would one type of matter warm up more than the other? How might you test your ideas?

Write a **Hypothesis:** _____

_____

_____

Materials

- soil
- water
- 2 foam cups
- 2 thermometers
- heat source (sunlight or lamp)

Procedures

1. Fill one of the cups with water. Place an equal amount of soil in the other cup.

2. **Measure** Using your thermometers, measure how warm the soil and water are. Record your measurements.

_____

3. Estimate how hot the soil and water will get if they are left in a warm place for 15 minutes. Record your estimates, then place the soil and water near a heat source. Make sure they are the same distance from the heat source.

_____

4. **Measure** Record the readings on the thermometers every

5 minutes for 15 minutes. _____

5. **Use Numbers** Find the difference between the first thermometer reading and the last. To do this, subtract the first measurement you made from the last measurement you made.

_____

Conclude and Apply

1. Identify Which type of matter warmed up more? How do you know?

_____

_____

2. Compare and Contrast Were your estimates close to your actual measurements?

_____

Going Further: Apply

3. Infer Why is it important to place the soil and water an equal distance from the heat source?

_____

_____

 **Inquiry**

Think of your own questions that you might test. Which would get hotter when they are exposed to the same amount of heat—sand or water?

My Question Is:

_____

How I Can Test It:

_____

_____

My Results Are:

_____

Expand and Contract

Hypothesize Do gases expand when heated? Do they contract when cooled?

Write a **Hypothesis:**

_____

_____

Materials

- balloon
- 2L plastic bottle
- bucket of warm water
- bucket of cool water

Procedures

1. Stretch the opening of the balloon over the opening of the bottle.

2. **Predict** What will happen when you place the bottle in the bucket of warm water? Test your prediction.

_____

_____

_____

_____

3. **Predict** What will happen when you place the bottle in the bucket of cool water? Test your prediction.

_____

_____

_____

_____

Conclude and Apply

1. **Communicate** What happened to the balloon when you placed it in warm water? In cold water?

_____

_____

_____

2. **Draw Conclusions** What happened to the air particles in the balloon when the bottle was in the warm water? The cool water?

_____

_____

_____

Going Further Does the size of the bottle affect how the balloon expands? Write and conduct an experiment.

My Hypothesis Is:

_____

My Experiment Is:

_____

_____

My Results Are:

_____

_____

Investigate What Materials Light Passes Through

Hypothesize What kinds of materials can light pass through? How might you test your ideas?

Write a **Hypothesis:**

_____

Test these materials to see which ones allow light to pass through.

Materials

• flashlight

• large balloon

• classroom materials

Procedures

1. **Experiment** Hold one material at a time in front of the lighted flashlight. Does the light shine through the material? Record your observations.

_____

_____

2. **Observe** Blow up your balloon. Look through the balloon. What do you observe now?

_____

3. **Experiment** Try changing the other materials in some way. You may want to fold the papers several times to make them thicker, or crumple up the plastic wrap. After you have made a change in the material, test the material again. Record both the change you made and any new observations.

_____

_____

_____

_____

Conclude and Apply

1. Classify Which materials did the light pass through? List them. Which materials blocked the light? Make a separate list of the materials.

_____

_____

2. Explain What was the effect of the change you made to each material?

_____

_____

_____

Going Further: Apply

3. Identify Look at the list of materials that light passed through. What properties do these materials have in common?

_____

_____

🔮 Inquiry

Think of your own questions that you might test. What other materials would you like to test?

My Question Is:

_____

How I Can Test It:

_____

My Results Are:

_____

Using Variables

Controlling an Experiment

Variables are things in an experiment that can be changed or controlled. For example, suppose you wanted to answer the question: *What affects how light bends in a liquid?* Here are some variables that could be changed:

- the kind of liquid you use
- the size of the container you use
- the position of the object in the liquid

Procedures

1. **Compare** Take a close look at the containers in the picture. What differences do you see? Describe them below. These differences are variables. List all the variables you can identify on the left side of the table on the next page. The first variable is given.

   _____

   _____

   _____

   _____

2. **Communicate** Complete the table. After you identify as many
   variables as you can, indicate how you could control each
   variable.

   _____

   _____

   _____

   _____

Variable	Control
Container	

Conclude and Apply

Identify Which one variable would you change to see its effect on
the bending of light? Why?

_____

_____

_____

_____

Investigate What Makes It Light

Hypothesize You often have to put parts together in a certain way for something to work. How can you put a light bulb, wire, and battery together so that the bulb lights? How might you test your ideas?

Write a **Hypothesis:**

_____

_____

Test what makes the bulb light by putting the parts together in different ways.

Materials

• D cell   • small light bulb   • 20 cm wire

Procedures

1. **Observe** Look at the bulb, wire, and cell. How do you think you might put these three things together to make the bulb light? Record any ideas you may have.

_____

_____

2. **Experiment** Try to light the bulb. Draw a picture of each set-up that you try on a separate sheet of paper. Record which ones work and which ones don't.

Conclude and Apply

1. **Identify** How many ways did you find to light the bulb? How many ways did you find that did not light the bulb?

_____

2. Compare and Contrast How were the ways that worked to light the bulb alike? How were they different from the ways that did not work?

_____

_____

_____

_____

Going Further: Apply

3. Draw Conclusions How must the bulb, wire, and cell be put together so that the bulb will light?

_____

_____

_____

Inquiry

Think of your own questions that you might test. Can you change your setup and still light the bulb?

My Question Is:

_____

How I Can Test It:

_____

My Results Are:

_____

Make a Flashlight

Hypothesize A flashlight is a source of light that uses cells as its source of electricity. How can you put the materials together to make a model of a flashlight?

Write a **Hypothesis:**

_____

_____

_____

_____

Materials

- 2 D cells
- paper tube
- 30 cm wire
- flashlight bulb

Procedures

Make a Model Use the materials provided for you to construct a model of a flashlight.

Conclude and Apply

1. **Explain** How is your model like a real flashlight? How is your model different?

_____

_____

_____

_____

_____

2. Communicate Draw a diagram of your model flashlight's circuit on a separate sheet of paper. How are you able to turn your circuit on and off?

_____

_____

_____

Going Further Electricity can flow through some types of materials but not others. How can you use a circuit to find out whether electricity can flow through certain materials? Write and conduct an experiment.

My Hypothesis Is:

_____

_____

My Experiment Is:

_____

_____

_____

_____

My Results Are:

_____

_____

_____

Investigate What Causes Night and Day

Hypothesize The Sun gives us plenty of light during the day. Where does it go at night? How might you test your ideas?

Write a **Hypothesis:**

_____

Use a model to investigate what causes night and day.

Materials

• 2 to 5 medium self-stick notes   • globe   • flashlight

Procedures

1. **Make a Model** Write "I live here" on a self-stick note. Place it over the United States on the globe. Pick another place on the opposite side of the globe. It can be where a friend lives. Write "My friend lives here" and place it on the globe.

2. In a darkened room, one person will hold the globe, or Earth. Another person will hold the flashlight, or the Sun. The third person will record the results.

3. **Observe** Shine the light on the globe at the place where you live. Is it day or night where you live? Is it day or night where your friend lives?

_____

_____

_____

4. **Experiment** Think of two different ways to make it night where you live. Use the globe and the flashlight to show both of your ideas. Record your observations.

_____

_____

Conclude and Apply

1. **Explain** What was the first way you made day turn into night? The second way?

_____

_____

2. **Compare and Contrast** How do your group's ideas compare with other groups?

_____

_____

Going Further: Apply

3. **Identify** Which example do you think best explains what you know about day and night? Why?

_____

_____

? Inquiry

Think of your own questions that you might like to test. How can you tell in which country it is nighttime now?

My Question Is:

_____

How I Can Test It:

_____

_____

My Results Are:

_____

Sundial

Hypothesize How can you measure the Sun's changing path in the sky?

Write a **Hypothesis:**

_____

_____

Materials

- pencil
- marker
- paper taped to cardboard
- clay

Procedures

1. At 9 A.M. on a sunny day, go outside with your materials. Working on the ground, use the clay to anchor the pencil to the center of the paper.

2. **Measure** Use the marker to draw a line straight through the middle of the pencil's shadow. Label the line with the time of day. Measure the pencil's shadow again at 12 P.M. and 3 P.M. Label the paper with the date.

3. **Repeat** Once a month, measure the pencil's shadow three times a day. Label each paper with the date you make your measurements.

Conclude and Apply

1. **Compare and Contrast** How does the position of the pencil's shadow change throughout one day? Is the Sun high or low in the sky when the shadows are the longest?

_____

_____

_____

2. **Infer** During which month is the Sun's path highest in the sky? Lowest? How do you know?

_____

_____

_____

Going Further Shadows are shorter and longer at different times of the day. What time of the day is your shadow the longest and the shortest? Write and conduct an experiment.

My Hypothesis Is:

_____

_____

My Experiment Is:

_____

_____

My Results Are:

_____

_____

Investigate How the Moon's Shape Changes

Hypothesize You know that the Moon does not always look the same. Can a sphere look like a different shape without actually changing its shape?

Write a **Hypothesis:**

_____

_____

Use a model to investigate how a sphere can appear to change its shape.

Materials

• lamp   • white volleyball

Procedures

1. **Observe** Look closely at the ball from your seat. Draw the ball on a separate sheet of paper.

2. Next turn off the classroom lights. Turn on the lamp and shine it on one side of the ball. On your paper, draw the shape of the ball where the light is hitting it.

3. **Communicate** Share your drawing with the rest of the class.

4. **Infer** Compare all the drawings. What do you think caused the

    different shapes? _____

_____

Conclude and Apply

1. **Compare** How did the ball look when you first observed it? How did it look in the darkened room?

_____

_____

2. Compare How did your drawing compare with those of
your classmates?

_____

_____

Going Further: Apply

3. Draw Conclusions How did the round ball appear to be a
different shape without really changing its shape?

_____

_____

Inquiry

Think of your own questions that you might like to test using the lamp
and volleyball. What would happen if you changed the position of the
lamp or ball?

My Question Is:

_____

_____

How I Can Test It:

_____

_____

My Results Are:

_____

_____

Predicting

Using Patterns

Rachel observed the Moon on different days over one month. She drew her observations on this calendar. There were some days she did not observe the Moon. Can you predict the shape of the Moon on the days she did not observe?

SEPTEMBER						
Sunday	Monday	Tuesday	Wednesday	Thursday	Friday	Saturday
		1	2	3	4	5
6	7	8	9	10	11	12
13	14	15	16	17	18	19
20	21	22	23	24	25	26
27	28	29				

Materials

• markers

Procedures

1. **Observe** Study the drawings Rachel made of her observations of the Moon.

2. Look for similar shapes and patterns of the Moon.

Conclude and Apply

1. **Predict** What do you think the Moon's shape was on Wednesday, September 9th? Compare it to the shape of the Moon on the 8th and the 11th. Draw your prediction on the calendar above.

Name _____ SKILL BUILDER 2

Predicting Page 2

2.Compare and Contrast What was the Moon's shape on Friday, September 25th? Compare the shape of the Moon on the 24th and the 26th. Draw the shape of the Moon on the 25th on the calendar.

_____

_____

_____

3. Predict On the calendar, draw the shape of the Moon you would expect to see on the 29th. What helped you decide on that shape?

_____

_____

_____

_____

4. Communicate What helps you predict moon shapes? What do you need to know to predict the shape of tomorrow's Moon?

_____

_____

_____

_____

McGraw-Hill Science Unit: THE SUN AND ITS FAMILY

Investigate the Sizes of the Sun and the Moon

Hypothesize The Sun and the Moon appear to be the same size in the sky. One is actually larger. Why do you think they look the same size?

Write a **Hypothesis:**

_____

_____

Use a model to investigate why the Sun and the Moon appear to be the same size in the sky.

Materials

• notched index card   • meter tape or stick
• 1-inch styrofoam ball, 2-inch styrofoam ball, 3-inch styrofoam ball

Procedures

1. **Measure** Place the 1-inch and the 3-inch balls in a line across a table 10 cm from the edge. Bend down so that your eyes are at table-top level. Look at the balls through the notch in the index card. How do their sizes compare? Write your observations.

_____

2. **Experiment** Place the 1-inch ball at the edge of the table. Move the 3-inch ball back on the table until it appears to be the same size as the 1-inch ball.

3. **Predict** Where would you have to place the 2-inch ball so that its size appears to be the same as the other balls? Test your prediction.

_____

_____

Conclude and Apply

1. **Explain** What did you observe as each ball moved farther from your eyes?

_____

2. Identify Where did you place the 2-inch ball so that it seemed to
be the same size as the others?

_____

Going Further: Apply

3. Infer The Sun and the Moon appear to be the same size in the sky.
The Sun is much farther from Earth than the Moon. Are the Sun
and the Moon really the same size? Why does it look that way?

_____

_____

_____

 Inquiry

Think of your own questions that you might like to test using the three
styrofoam balls. What would happen if the Moon or Sun were closer
to Earth?

My Question Is:

_____

_____

How I Can Test It:

_____

_____

My Results Are:

_____

_____

It's Farther Than You Think!

Hypothesize How can you model the distance from Earth to the Sun?

Write a **Hypothesis:**

_____

_____

Materials

• construction paper, 4½" x 6"   • markers

                                    • meter tape

Procedures

1. Make signs with construction paper. Write "Earth" on one sign, "Moon" on another, and "Sun" on the third.

2. **Measure** Have one person hold the sign labeled "Earth." Another person will hold the Sun sign 75 m away from the Earth sign. Have someone hold the Moon sign 19 cm away from the Earth sign.

3. **Observe** Look at the distances between the Sun, Earth, and the Moon. Change positions so everyone gets a chance to observe the model.

Name _____ QUICK LAB 3

It's Farther Than You Think! Page 2

Conclude and Apply

Compare How do the Sun and the Moon compare in their distance from Earth?

_____

Going Further The Sun and the Moon are different distances from Earth, but look the same size. Is one larger than the other? Write and conduct an experiment.

My Hypothesis Is:

_____

My Experiment Is:

_____

_____

My Results Are:

_____

_____

Investigate How the Sun's Energy Affects Earth

Hypothesis Each day Earth receives light and heat from the Sun. How does this affect Earth's temperature?

Write a **Hypothesis:**

_____

_____

Use a model to explore how the Sun's energy affects Earth's temperature.

Materials

- lamp with light bulb, 60 watt
- meter stick
- black paper
- thermometer
- aluminum can
- tape

Procedures

1. **Make a Model** Cover the can with black paper. The can represents Earth. Place the thermometer in the can, and set the can on a table 20 cm from the lamp. The lamp represents the Sun.

2. **Collect Data** Read the temperature inside the can. Record the number in a table on a separate sheet of paper.

3. **Collect Data** Turn on the lamp. Record the temperature of the can every two minutes for 10 minutes.

Conclude and Apply

1. **Identify** What was your first temperature measurement? What was the temperature after 10 minutes?

_____

_____

2. Explain Was the temperature of the can still increasing after 10 minutes? How do you know?

_____

3. Infer Why did the temperature of the can stop increasing? Where do you think the energy from the lamp is going?

_____

_____

Going Further: Problem Solving

4. Experiment Suppose the can was twice as far from the lamp. How warm do you think it would get in 10 minutes? Write your prediction. Test it.

_____

 Inquiry

Think of your own questions that you might like to test using the light bulb, can, and thermometer. What would happen if the Sun were closer to Earth?

My Question Is:

_____

_____

How I Can Test It:

_____

_____

My Results Are:

_____

_____

Compare the Sun and the Moon

Hypothesize How are the Sun and the Moon alike?
How are they different?

Write a **Hypothesis:**

_____

_____

_____

_____

Procedures

1. With your partner, list as many facts as you can about the Sun
   and the Moon on a separate sheet of paper.

2. **Identify** Separate the things that are similar about the Sun and
   the Moon from the things that are different.

Conclude and Apply

Communicate Organize your facts into a chart comparing the
Sun and the Moon. Make your chart in the space below. Illustrate
your chart.

Going Further If you could choose between exploring the Sun and the Moon, which would you choose? Why? Write and conduct an experiment.

My Hypothesis Is:

_____

My Experiment Is:

_____

_____

My Results Are:

_____

_____

Investigate How Planets Move

Hypothesize You know that the Moon appears to change shape as it moves around Earth. You can observe other changes in the night sky, too—like the position of the planets. Why don't you see the planets in the same place every night?

Write a **Hypothesis:**

_____

_____

Use a model to investigate the motion of the planets.

Materials

- sign for each planet
- 2 signs for the Sun

Procedures

1. **Make a Model** The class will be divided into two groups. The first group will model the motion of the planets around the Sun. The second group will observe. Then the second group will model and the first group will observe.

2. **Observe** Listen to the student who is modeling Earth. He or she will share with the class what can be seen from Earth in the night sky. Record your observations on a separate sheet of paper.

Conclude and Apply

1. **Compare** Which planets were visible from Earth the first time you modeled the motions of the planets? Which planets were visible from Earth the second time?

_____

_____

2. **Explain** How did Earth's motion affect which planets could be seen from Earth? How did the motion of the other planets affect which planets could be seen from Earth?

_____

_____

3. **Draw Conclusions** Why does the position of the planets in the night sky change?

_____

_____

Going Further: Apply

4. **Predict** What would happen if you had moved faster around the Sun? If you had moved more slowly?

_____

_____

Inquiry

Think of your own questions that you might like to test using the signs for the Sun and the planets. If you lived on another planet, which planets can be seen from your home in the night sky?

My Question Is:

_____

How I Can Test It:

_____

_____

My Results Are:

_____

Make a Letter Larger

Hypothesize How does the shape of lenses change how objects look?

Write a **Hypothesis:**

_____

Materials

- dropper
- newspaper
- water

- masking tape
- paper cup
- wax paper

Procedures

1. Lay the newspaper flat and cover it with wax paper. Tape the wax paper down over the newspaper.

2. **Observe** Put a small drop of water over a printed letter. How does the print look under the water drop?

_____

3. **Experiment** Put water drops of different sizes over other letters. Look at the shape of each letter.

Conclude and Apply

1. **Compare** Are big drops and small drops of water shaped the same? How does the size of the drop affect the way the print looks?

_____

_____

_____

2. Infer How do you think the curved lens in a telescope might be like the drop of water on the wax paper?

_____

_____

Going Further What if you could magnify something tiny. What would it be? Write and conduct an experiment.

My Hypothesis Is:

_____

My Experiment Is:

_____

_____

My Results Are:

_____

_____

Design Your Own Experiment

What Is the Volume of Jupiter?

Hypothesize How might you use a model to compare the volumes of Jupiter and Earth?

Write a **Hypothesis:**

_____

_____

_____

Materials

• 2 lb. bag of beans
• plastic bowl
• small cup

Procedures

1. If Earth had the volume of a bean, Jupiter would have the volume of the bowl.

2. **Make a Model** How can you estimate how much larger the volume of the bowl is than the volume of the bean?

3. **Communicate** Write your plan. Share your plan with your teacher.

_____

_____

_____

_____

_____

4. **Experiment** Try your plan.

Conclude and Apply

1. Use Numbers How much greater is the volume of the bowl than the

volume of the bean? _____

2. Draw Conclusions How much greater is the volume of Jupiter than

the volume of Earth? _____

_____

Going Further: Apply

3. Infer How do the spaces between the beans in the bowl affect your

estimate? _____

_____

_____

 **Inquiry**

Think of your own questions that you might like to test using the
beans, cup, and bowl. How might you make a more accurate estimate?

My Question Is:

_____

_____

How I Can Test It:

_____

_____

_____

My Results Are:

_____

Inferring

Using Observations to Explain an Event

Why does Jupiter's ring shine? In this activity you will make a model to show what happens when light shines on dust particles. You can use what you observe to suggest an explanation of why Jupiter's ring shines. When you suggest an explanation for an event based on observations you have made, you are inferring. To infer means to form an idea from facts or observations.

Materials

- flashlight
- newspaper
- plastic bottle of cornstarch
- safety goggles

Procedures

Safety Wear goggles.

1. Place the flashlight on the edge of a table. Cover the area below the table with newspaper. Darken the room.

2. **Observe** Turn on the flashlight. What do you see? Record your observations.

_____

3. **Observe** Holding the opened bottle of cornstarch below the beam of light, quickly squeeze the bottle. What do you see?

_____

_____

Conclude and Apply

1. **Compare** How did the beam of light appear when you first observed it? How did it appear after you squeezed the cornstarch into it?

_____

_____

_____

_____

2. **Infer** Jupiter's ring is made up of dust particles. Why do you think Jupiter's ring shines?

_____

_____

_____

Investigate How Rocks Are Alike and Different

Hypothesize What makes up rocks? Are all rocks alike? How might you test your ideas?

Write a **Hypothesis:**

_____

_____

Observe different rocks to infer how they are alike and different.

Materials

• several different rocks   • hand lens

Procedures

1. **Observe** Touch each rock. How does it feel? Record your observations.

_____

_____

2. **Observe** Look at each rock. Write or draw what you see on another sheet of paper. Write about any lines or patterns you observe.

3. **Compare** Now use your hand lens to look at each rock again. Write about what you see with the hand lens that you could not see before on the same sheet of paper.

Conclude and Apply

1. **Compare and Contrast** Did any rocks feel the same? Did any rocks have similar lines or patterns?

_____

_____

_____

2. Identify When you observed the rocks with a hand lens, did you observe any quality that all the rocks have in common?

_____

3. Infer Are the rocks made of one material or more than one material? How can you tell?

_____

_____

Going Further: Apply

4. Classify Based on your observations, what are some ways the rocks could be grouped together to show their similarities or differences?

_____

_____

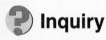 **Inquiry**

Think of your own questions that you might like to test. How else are rocks alike or different?

My Question Is:

_____

How I Can Test It:

_____

_____

My Results Are:

_____

_____

Mineral Scratch Test

Hypothesize Which of these minerals do you think is the hardest: quartz, calcite, or mica?

Write a **Hypothesis:**

_____

Materials

- large pieces of quartz, calcite, and mica
- penny
- iron nail

Procedures

1. **Predict** What do you think will happen if you scratch each mineral with your fingernail? The penny? The iron nail? Write your predictions.

   _____

   _____

   _____

   _____

2. **Observe** Test your predictions. Scratch each mineral with your fingernail, the penny, and the iron nail. Record your observations.

   _____

   _____

   _____

Conclude and Apply

1. **Interpret Data** List the minerals you tested in order of hardness, from softest to hardest. How did you determine the order?

_____

_____

_____

2. **Communicate** Use your observations to create a chart that describes the three minerals you tested. Include drawings of the minerals.

Going Further Think of your own questions you might like to test. Can any of the three rocks scratch each other?

My Question Is:

_____

How I Can Test It:

_____

My Results Are:

_____

_____

Investigate How Rocks Change

Hypothesize Chalk is a kind of rock made up of the mineral calcite. How do you think the chalk got its shape? What are some ways you could change its shape? How might you test your ideas?

Write a **Hypothesis:**

_____

_____

Investigate how rocks can change. Test what happens to chalk when you write on sandpaper.

Materials

• 3 pieces of chalk (different colors)   • piece of sandpaper

Procedures

1. **Observe** Look at your piece of chalk and your sandpaper. Write down what they look and feel like. On another sheet of paper, list as many properties of each one as you can.

2. **Predict** What will happen when you draw with the chalk on the sandpaper? Write down your prediction.

_____

_____

3. Draw with your chalk on the sandpaper. You might draw a picture or write some words.

4. **Compare** Look at your chalk. How does the way it looks and feels now compare to before? Look at your sandpaper. How does the way it looks and feels now compare to before? Record your observations on another sheet of paper.

Name _____

Conclude and Apply

1. **Describe** What happened to the piece of chalk?
   What happened to the sandpaper?

   _____

   _____

2. **Explain** Which material changed the most? Why do you think
   this happened?

   _____

   _____

Going Further: Apply

3. **Infer** Strong winds sometimes carry sand as they blow over
   rocks. How might the wind and sand change the rocks over time?

   _____

❓ Inquiry

Think of your own questions that you might like to test. How else
might rocks be worn down?

My Question Is:

_____

How I Can Test It:

_____

_____

My Results Are:

_____

_____

Changing Chalk

Hypothesize Vinegar is a kind of chemical. What will happen when chalk is put in vinegar?

Write a **Hypothesis:**

_____

Materials

- apron
- safety goggles
- piece of chalk
- small jar
- vinegar

Procedures

Safety Wear goggles.

1. Put on your apron and safety goggles. Place the chalk in the jar and pour in just enough vinegar to cover the chalk.

2. **Observe** After a few seconds, describe what you see. Record your observations.

_____

_____

Conclude and Apply

Explain Why did the chalk change? How do you know?

_____

_____

_____

Going Further Think of your own questions you might like to test.
Would adding other liquids have the same effect on chalk as vinegar
alone?

My Question Is:

_____

_____

How I Can Test It:

_____

_____

My Results Are:

_____

_____

Skill: Forming a Hypothesis

Which Materials Settle First?

What happens to the material that is carried away by erosion? In this activity, you will put pebbles, sand, soil, and water in a jar. After you shake the jar, you will let it sit for several hours. How will the materials in the jar look after several hours? Write down what you think the outcome will be. This is your hypothesis. A hypothesis is an answer you propose to a question that can be tested.

My **Hypothesis:**

_____

Materials

- a large plastic jar with lid
- measuring cup
- pebbles

- sand
- soil
- water

Procedures

1. Put one cup of each of the materials (pebbles, sand, and soil) in the jar and fill the jar with water. Put the lid on the jar and shake it.

2. **Observe** Write a description of what your jar looks like. Draw a picture of the jar and the materials in the space below.

_____

_____

_____

3. Observe Let the jar sit for several hours, then observe the contents again. How does the jar look now?

_____

_____

_____

Conclude and Apply

1. Compare How did the jar look when you first observed it? How did it look several hours later? Was your hypothesis correct?

_____

_____

_____

_____

2. Describe Which material in the jar settled first? Last? How do you know?

_____

_____

_____

3. Infer A fast-moving stream may carry pebbles, sand, and soil. As the water slows down, which material will settle out first? Which material will be carried the greatest distance?

_____

_____

_____

Design Your Own Experiment

How Can Land Change Quickly?

Hypothesize A hurricane is a powerful storm. A drizzle isn't a storm at all. Each dumps water on land. Which kind of rainfall causes the most erosion? How might you test your ideas?

Write a **Hypothesis:**

_____

_____

Materials

- 2 paper cups, labeled A and B
- 2 different-sized pencils
- soil and rocks

- 2 trays, labeled A and B
- measuring cup
- water

Procedures

1. Mix some rocks and soil together. You can smooth the rocks and soil or shape them into a hill, but don't pack them down. Draw how your "land" looks on a separate sheet of paper.

2. **Model** How can you use cups A and B to model a gentle rain and a heavy rain? How can you use the pencils to help you?

_____

_____

_____

3. **Experiment** How is your land affected by a gentle rain? How is your land affected by a heavy rain?

_____

_____

Conclude and Apply

1. **Compare** What happened to the two trays? In which tray did the most change take place?

   _____

   _____

2. **Draw Conclusions** Which kind of rainfall causes the most erosion? How do you know?

   _____

   _____

   _____

   _____

Going Further: Problem Solving

3. **Experiment** How could you test the effects of wind on land?

   _____

   _____

❓ Inquiry

Think of your own questions that you might like to test. How else might you test the effects of natural events on land?

My Question Is:

_____

How I Can Test It:

_____

_____

My Results Are:

_____

Weather Adds Up

Hypothesize Some cities have a lot of rain each year. Other cities only have a little. In which kind of city will a stone monument change more quickly?

_____

_____

COMPARING WEATHER IN NEW YORK AND CAIRO		
	New York City, USA	**Cairo, Egypt**
Average Temperature in Winter	32°F	56°F
Average Rainfall Each Year	107 cm	0 to 10 cm

Procedures

1. **Interpret Data** Look at the table. What is the difference in winter temperatures between the two cities? Write the number.

_____

2. **Interpret Data** Which city has more rainfall?

_____

Conclude and Apply

Draw Conclusions A stone monument was moved to New York City
from Egypt. The monument has changed very quickly in New York.
Why do you think this has happened?

_____

_____

_____

_____

_____

Going Further Think of your own questions that you might like to
test. Does what a monument is made of have an effect on how much
it changes?

My Question Is:

_____

_____

How I Can Test It:

_____

_____

_____

My Results Are:

_____

Investigate What Is in Soil

Hypothesize You know that soil is important for growing plants. What is in soil? How might you test your ideas?

Write a **Hypothesis:**

_____

_____

Examine a soil sample to find out what is in soil.

Materials

- small amount of soil
- piece of white paper
- hand lens

Procedures

1. Spread out your soil sample on the piece of white paper.

2. **Observe** Look at the soil closely. What do you see? Are there different colors? Different size particles? Write your observations.

_____

_____

3. **Observe** Smell your soil. How does it smell? Feel your soil. How does it feel? Are there different textures? Write down a description of your soil based on how it looks, feels, and smells. Be sure to wash your hands after touching the soil.

_____

_____

4. **Compare** Using your hand lens, examine your soil again. What do you see that you didn't see before? Record your new observations.

_____

_____

Conclude and Apply

1. Communicate What did you see in your soil?

_____

_____

2. Identify Was there anything in the soil that surprised you? What was it?

_____

_____

Going Further: Apply

3. Hypothesize Think about what you saw in your soil. How do you think those things got into the soil?

_____

_____

❓ Inquiry

Think of your own questions that you might like to test. How is soil different in different places?

My Question Is:

_____

How I Can Test It:

_____

_____

My Results Are:

_____

_____

McGraw-Hill Science Unit: ROCKS AND RESOURCES

Skill: Measuring

Finding the Volume of a Water Sample

The amount of water that soil can hold is an important property of
soil. In this activity, you will measure the amount of water held by two
soil samples. Sometimes you measure something to find out an
object's size, weight, or temperature. In this activity, you will measure
the volume of a sample of water. You can use a calculator to help.

Materials

- 4 paper cups, 2 with holes
- water
- potting soil
- watch or clock

- measuring cup
- sandy soil
- graduated cylinder
- calculator (optional)

Procedures

1. **Measure** Using the measuring cup, measure 1 cup of potting soil
   into a paper cup with holes. Pack the soil down. Label the cup.
   Measure 100 mL of water in the graduated cylinder.

2. **Experiment** Hold the paper cup with potting soil over a paper cup
   without holes. Have your partner pour the water slowly into the cup
   of soil. Let the water run through the cup for two minutes. If there is
   still water dripping out, place the cup of soil inside an empty cup.

3. **Measure** Pour the water that ran out of the cup into the
   graduated cylinder. Read and record the volume of water in
   the graduated cylinder.

   _____

   _____

4. **Experiment** Repeat steps 1–3 with the sandy soil.

   _____

   _____

Conclude and Apply

1. Interpret Which soil held more water? How do you know?

_____

_____

_____

_____

_____

2. Apply Which type of soil would be best for use in a garden? Which sample would be best for use on a soccer field?

_____

_____

_____

_____

_____

Investigate How Mining Affects Land

Hypothesize Some natural resources, such as diamonds and metals, are hard to find. What effect do you think mining these resources might have on Earth's land? How might you use a model to test your ideas?

Write a **Hypothesis:**

_____

_____

The cookie in this activity represents an area of land. The chocolate chips in the cookie are the resource. Experiment to find out what you must do to get the resource.

Materials

• chocolate chip cookie   • 4 toothpicks   • paper towel

Procedures

1. **Observe** Place your cookie on the paper towel. Draw how your cookie looks on another sheet of paper. Label your drawing.

2. **Model** Using your toothpicks, try to remove the resource (chocolate chips) from the land (cookie) without damaging the land. Before you begin, discuss with your partner how you will mine the resource.

3. **Experiment** Mine all the resource from your land. Draw how your cookie looks now.

Conclude and Apply

1. **Compare** How does your cookie look after you removed all the chocolate chips?

_____

_____

2. Draw Conclusions What happens when you can't find any more chips? How can you get more?

_____

_____

3. Infer What might be some problems people face in trying to mine resources from Earth?

_____

_____

_____

Going Further: Problem Solving

4. How can damage to mining areas be repaired?

_____

_____

_____

Inquiry

Think of your own questions that you might like to test. How much harder is it to mine underneath the surface of Earth than on its surface?

My Question Is:

_____

_____

How I Can Test It:

_____

My Results Are:

_____

_____

Energy Survey

Hypothesize Do you think more people in your class have a gas stove or an electric stove?

Write a **Hypothesis:**

_____

_____

Procedures

Collect Data Conduct a survey of your classmates. Who has an electric stove? Who has a gas stove? Record the information in the table below.

Students with Electric Stoves	Students with Gas Stoves

Conclude and Apply

1. **Identify** How many people have electric stoves? How many people have gas stoves?

_____

_____

2. **Communicate** On a separate sheet of paper, make a bar graph that shows the results of your survey.

Going Further Think about your own questions that you might like to test. What other appliances that can be powered by either gas or electricity can you collect data on?

My Question Is:

_____

_____

How I Can Test It:

_____

_____

My Results Are:

_____

Investigate What Happens When Materials Get into Water

Hypothesize One way we use water is to keep ourselves clean. When you wash your hands, where do the dirt and grime go? Do they stay in the water? How might you test your ideas?

Write a **Hypothesis:**

_____

_____

Explore what happens when materials are put into water.

Materials

- small jar with lid
- plastic spoon
- water
- oil
- liquid soap
- safety goggles

Procedures   Safety Wear goggles.

1. **Observe** Pour some water into your jar and add a spoonful of the oil. How does the water look? Where is the oil? Record your observations.

_____

2. **Observe** Shake the jar. Set the jar down and watch it for a few minutes. What happens? Can you scoop the oil out with your spoon?

_____

_____

3. **Experiment** Add a few drops of liquid soap to the jar and shake the jar again. What happened to the oil? Can you clean the oil out now?

_____

_____

Conclude and Apply

1. Describe What happened when you shook the jar with the oil and water in it?

_____

_____

2. Identify Where did the oil and soap go when you shook the jar a second time?

_____

_____

Going Further: Apply

3. Infer Where do you think dirt and grime go when you wash a car or dirty dishes?

_____

_____

_____

🔵 Inquiry

Think of your own questions that you might like to test. How much soap does it take to clean out oil?

My Question Is:

_____

How I Can Test It:

_____

My Results Are:

_____

Cleaning Water

Hypothesize Can you clean water by letting it flow through rocks?

Write a **Hypothesis:**

_____

_____

Materials

- plastic funnel
- gravel
- measuring cup
- spoonful of soil
- cup
- bottom half of plastic bottle
- sand
- water
- dead leaf
- safety goggles

Procedures

Safety Wear goggles.

1. **Model** Place the funnel inside the bottom half of the plastic bottle. Put a layer of gravel in the funnel and cover it with a layer of sand.

2. **Model** Mix a cup of water with a little soil and some crushed leaves. Draw a picture of the water in the space below. Slowly pour the mixture into the funnel.

Conclude and Apply

1. Describe How does the water look when it filters through to the bottom half of the bottle?

_____

2. Infer Where is the soil?

_____

Going Further Think of your own questions that you might like to test. Does the amount of sand and gravel affect what happens to the water?

My Question Is:

_____

_____

How I Can Test It:

_____

_____

My Results Are:

_____

_____

Investigate Where Plants and Animals Live

Hypothesize Why do organisms live where they do?

Write a **Hypothesis:** _____

_____

Explore why plants and animals live where they do.

Materials

• magazines   • scissors

Procedures

1. Using the magazines and scissors, cut out pictures of 4 different environments. Look for pictures of deserts, forests, ponds, and grasslands. Spread the pictures on a table.

2. **Observe** Cut out 8 pictures of different plants and animals and trade them for the plant and animal pictures cut out by another group. Look at the pictures carefully. To which environment do you think each plant or animal is best suited for survival? Give reasons for your choices.

Plant or Animal	Environment	Reasons

3. Make Decisions Place the plant and animal pictures under the environment you have chosen for them.

Conclude and Apply

1. **Identify** What are the characteristics of the organisms that live in each environment? Make a list.

_____

_____

_____

_____

Going Further: Apply

2. **Infer** What determines where organisms live?

_____

_____

Inquiry

Think of your own questions that you might like to test. What kinds of organisms live in your environment?

My Question Is:

_____

How I Can Test It:

_____

_____

My Results Are:

_____

Defining Terms Based on Observations

A Forest Community

You have learned that a community is all the living things in an ecosystem. Different ecosystems have different communities. For example, the pond community on pages 326 and 327 in your textbook included bladderwort, frogs, algae, and dragonflies. What makes up a forest community? Look at the picture on this page. Use your observations to define a forest community.

Procedures

1. Observe Look at the illustration of a forest. What do you see? Make a list.

_____

_____

_____

_____

2. Classify Which of the things on your list are living?
Which are nonliving?

Living Things	Nonliving Things

Conclude and Apply

Define Using your lists, define a forest community.

_____

_____

_____

_____

_____

_____

Investigate Where Food Comes From

Hypothesize People eat many different kinds of foods. Does more of the food you eat come from plants or animals? How might you investigate your ideas?

Write a **Hypothesis:**

_____

_____

Analyze a pizza to infer where food comes from.

Procedures

1. **Observe** Look carefully at the picture of the pizza. What types of food do you see? Make a list.

   _____

   _____

2. **Classify** Divide your list of foods into groups. Which foods come from plants? Which foods come from animals?

   _____

   _____

   _____

3. Plants can make their own food. Animals cannot. Look at your list of foods that come from animals. What animal does each of the foods come from? What food does that animal eat?

   _____

   _____

   _____

Conclude and Apply

1. **Cause and Effect** If there were no plants, which foods would be
left to make pizza? (**Hint:** Think about what animals eat in order
to survive.) _____

_____

_____

2. **Infer** Do all foods come from plants? Write down another type of food
that you like to eat. See if you can trace the ingredients back to plants.

_____

_____

_____

Going Further: Apply

3. **Communicate** Create a chart on a separate sheet of paper that
shows where the ingredients in question 2 come from.

 Inquiry

Think of your own questions that you might like to test.
Could you eat a diet based only on plants?

My Question Is:

_____

How I Can Test It:

_____

_____

My Results Are:

_____

_____

Decomposers

Hypothesize What will happen to bread and apples if they are left out for one week?

Write a **Hypothesis:**

_____

_____

Materials

- 2 self-sealing plastic bags
- apple pieces
- slice of bread

Safety Don't open the sealed bags.

Procedures

1. Put the bread in one plastic bag. Put the apple pieces in the other bag. Seal the bags.

2. **Observe** Leave the materials in the bags for one week. What happens to each material?

_____

_____

_____

_____

_____

_____

Conclude and Apply

1. Identify What evidence of decomposers do you see?
Is there more than one decomposer? How do you know?

_____

_____

_____

2. Infer Do different types of decomposers break down different
types of material? Explain.

_____

_____

_____

Going Further Think of your own questions that you might like to
test. What other materials will decomposers break down?

My Question Is:

_____

How I Can Test It:

_____

_____

My Results Are:

_____

Investigate How Living Things Meet Their Needs

Hypothesize Pets and houseplants have people to take care of them. How do plants and animals in nature get what they need to live and grow? How might you test your ideas?

Write a **Hypothesis:**

_____

_____

Observe an aquarium to infer how plants and animals meet their needs.

Materials

- fish food
- gravel
- small guppy or goldfish
- fish net
- 2 small elodea or other water plants
- 2 L plastic drink bottle
- bottom of another drink bottle with holes
- water
- meter tape

Procedures

1. **Make a Model** Put a 3 cm layer of gravel into the plastic drink bottle. Fill the bottle about half full of water. Anchor the plants by gently pushing their roots into the gravel. Cover the bottle with the bottom of another bottle. Put the container in a place where it receives plenty of light, but do not place it directly in the Sun.

2. After 2 days, use the fish net to gently place the fish into the bottle. Add a few flakes of fish food to the bottle through one of the holes in the top. Later in the week, add some more.

3. **Observe** Observe your ecosystem every few days for 4 weeks. Feed the fish twice each week. Record your observations on a separate sheet of paper.

Conclude and Apply

1. **Compare** How has your ecosystem changed over the 4 weeks?

_____

2. Identify What did the fish need to survive? What did the plants need to survive?

_____

_____

_____

3. Infer You probably observed bubbles in your ecosystem. What do you think those bubbles were? Where did they come from?

_____

Going Further: Apply

4. Infer Did the living things in this ecosystem meet their needs? How do you know?

_____

❓ Inquiry

Think of your own questions that you might like to test. What kind of food do fish eat?

My Question Is:

_____

How I Can Test It:

_____

My Results Are:

_____

Traveling Seeds

Hypothesize Animals with fur often help plants spread their seeds. How might they do this?

Write a **Hypothesis:**

_____

_____

Materials

• seeds
• fake fur

Procedures

1. **Predict** What will happen when you toss the seeds onto the fur? Record your prediction.

_____

2. **Experiment** Test your prediction. Have your partner hold up the fur. Toss different seeds at it. Record the results.

_____

_____

Conclude and Apply

1. **Identify** Which of the seeds stuck to the fur?

_____

_____

_____

2. **Infer** How might animals with fur help plants spread their seeds?

_____

_____

_____

Going Further Think of your own questions that you might like to test. What animal behaviors cause them to have seeds stuck to their fur?

My Question Is:

_____

_____

How I Can Test It:

_____

_____

My Results Are:

_____

_____

Investigate How Much Room Plants Need

Hypothesize You know that space is one of the needs of living things. When there are too many people in one place, it gets uncomfortable! What happens when there are too many plants in one place? Does the amount of space available affect the way plants grow?

Write a **Hypothesis:**

_____

_____

Explore how crowding affects how plants grow.

Materials

- soil
- water
- bean seeds
- masking tape
- scissors
- marker
- measuring cup
- 4 milk cartons

Procedures

1. Cut the tops from the milk cartons. Use the masking tape and the marker to label the cartons A to D. Carefully punch 3 drainage holes in the bottom of each carton. Use the measuring cup to fill each carton with the same amount of soil.

2. **Use Variables** Plant 3 bean seeds in carton A. Plant 6 bean seeds in carton B. Plant 12 bean seeds in carton C and 24 bean seeds in carton D.

3. **Predict** What do you think each carton will look like in 14 days? Draw a picture that shows your predictions on a separate sheet of paper.

4. **Experiment** Place the cartons in a well-lighted area. Water the plants every 2 days. Use the same amount of water for each carton.

Conclude and Apply

1. **Compare** How many plants are there in each carton? How do the plants in carton D compare to the plants in the other cartons?

_____

_____

2. Identify For what things are the plants in each container competing?

_____

3. Explain How did the number of plants in carton D affect the ability of each plant to get what it needs?

_____

_____

Going Further: Problem Solving

4. Experiment How could you test how much space pet gerbils need? Write a plan.

_____

_____

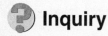 **Inquiry**

Think of your own questions that you might like to test using the soil, bean seeds, 4 milk cartons, and other materials from this activity. What would happen if these plants competed for only one of the things that they need to live?

My Question Is:

_____

_____

How I Can Test It:

_____

_____

My Results Are:

_____

_____

Musical Chairs

Hypothesize How does changing the number of chairs affect the game Musical Chairs?

Write a **Hypothesis:**

_____

_____

Materials

• chairs

Procedures

1. Play a game of Musical Chairs.

2. **Experiment** Change the number of chairs you play with. How does this affect the game? Record your observations.

_____

_____

Conclude and Apply

1. **Explain** What do the players compete for in Musical Chairs?

_____

2. **Identify** Why is there competition?

_____

_____

3. Compare and Contrast How is the competition in the game like competition in a real ecosystem? How is it different?

_____

_____

_____

Going Further Think of your own questions that you might like to test. How do people win the competition for chairs?

My Question Is:

_____

_____

How I Can Test It:

_____

_____

My Results Are:

_____

_____

Design Your Own Experiment

How Does the Shape of a Bird's Beak Affect What It Eats?

Hypothesize You know that animals are made up of different parts. All birds have beaks, but different kinds of birds have different kinds of beaks. How does a bird's beak help it eat the foods it needs?

Write a **Hypothesis:**

_____

_____

Materials

- chopsticks
- spoon
- tweezers

- rubber worm
- peanut in shell
- rice

- clothespin
- water in paper cup
- drinking straw

Procedures

1. **Plan** How can you model how a bird's beak helps it to eat? Look at the materials given to you. How will you use them? Record your plan.

_____

_____

2. **Collect Data** Follow your plan. Be sure to record all your observations. You might want to use the chart to record your data.

Tool	Food/Drink	Observations

Conclude and Apply

1. **Compare** Share your chart with other groups. How are your results similar? How are they different?

   _____

2. **Draw Conclusions** Are some tools better suited to different jobs? How do you know?

   _____

   _____

   _____

Going Further: Apply

3. **Infer** How might the shape of a bird's beak help it to eat the foods it needs?

   _____

   _____

Inquiry

Think of your own questions that you might like to test. Which tool is easiest to use to feed food to another person?

My Question Is:

_____

_____

How I Can Test It:

_____

My Results Are:

_____

Observing

Identifying Properties of an Environment

You know that camouflage is one way animals keep safe. In this activity you will observe an area of your classroom. When you observe something, you use one or more of your senses to learn about the properties of objects. You will use your observations of your classroom to help you design an animal that could hide in that environment.

Materials

- construction paper
- scissors
- yarn
- cotton balls
- crayons
- tape

Procedures

1. **Observe** Your teacher will help you select an area to observe. This area is the environment for the organism that you will design. What do you notice about the area? Record your observations.

   _____

   _____

   _____

   _____

2. **Plan** Discuss your observations with your group members. Make a list of features that would help an organism hide in this environment.

   _____

   _____

   _____

   _____

3. Use the materials given to you to create a plant or animal that will blend into its surroundings. Put your plant or animal into its environment.

Conclude and Apply

1. Observe Look for the organisms that your classmates designed. What are the features of each environment? Can you find the camouflaged organism? What characteristics help it to blend in?

_____

_____

_____

_____

_____

2. Communicate Describe the characteristics of the organism that you made. Explain why you included each one.

_____

_____

_____

_____

3. Infer Some animals can change the color of their body covering. When might they do this? Why?

_____

_____

_____

_____

_____

Investigate What Happens When Ecosystems Change

Hypothesize A big storm or volcanic eruption can cause a lot of change in a short amount of time. How do changes like these affect the living things in a particular area? How might you use a model to investigate your ideas?

Write a **Hypothesis:**

_____

Model what may happen when an ecosystem changes.

Materials

- 3 Predator cards: Red hawk, Blue owl, Green snake
- 12 Prey cards: 4 red, 4 blue, 4 green

Procedures

1. Make the 3 predator and 12 prey cards listed in the Materials. Give 1 predator card to each player. Stack the prey cards in the deck.

2. The object of the game is to get all 4 prey cards. To play:
   Predators take turns drawing a prey card from the deck.
   Keep prey cards that match the color of your predator card.
   Return all other prey cards to the pile. Play until one predator gets all 4 matching prey cards.

3. **Experiment** Add a card that says "fire" to the deck of prey cards. Play the game again. Any predator who draws the fire card must go out of the game. Return the fire card to the deck. The other two players continue to play until a predator gets all 4 prey cards or all players are out.

Conclude and Apply

1. **Compare and Contrast** What happened when you played the game the first time? What happened the second time?

   _____

   _____

2. Cause and Effect The fire card represented a change to the ecosystem. What effect did the change have?

_____

_____

3. Infer What may happen when an ecosystem changes?

_____

_____

Going Further: Problem Solving

4. Predict What might happen if you changed the number of prey cards?

_____

_____

_____

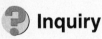 **Inquiry**

Think of your own questions that you might like to test using the cards. What would happen if you added another card to the game?

My Question Is:

_____

_____

How I Can Test It:

_____

My Results Are:

_____

_____

Crowd Control

Hypothesize What happens when the same number of organisms move into a smaller habitat?

Write a **Hypothesis:**

_____

_____

Materials

• 20 paper clips
• small box
• small book

Procedures

1. Toss the paper clips into the box. Remove any two paper clips that touch each other.

2. Gather the paper clips that remain from step 1 and toss them a second time. Again, remove all paper clips that touch. Repeat the process until all the paper clips are gone. Record the number of tosses you made.

_____

_____

3. **Experiment** Play the game again. This time put a book into the box to make the box smaller.

Conclude and Apply

Infer What happens when you crowd organisms together? How do their chances of survival change?

_____

_____

_____

Going Further Think about your own questions that you might like to test. What happens to the organisms if a new predator lives in the smaller habitat?

My Question Is:

_____

_____

How I Can Test It:

_____

_____

_____

_____

My Results Are:

_____

_____

Design Your Own Experiment

What Does Skin Do?

Hypothesize Your skin does more than cover your body. What other jobs do you think it does? How might you examine your skin to investigate what its jobs are?

Write a **Hypothesis:**

_____

_____

Materials

• water   • hand lens

Procedures

1. **Observe** How can you use your senses to find out more about your skin? You might record how your skin feels when you touch it, breathe on it, or blow on it.

_____

2. **Observe** How can you use the hand lens to observe your skin? What do you see? Record your observations. Draw what you see on a separate sheet of paper.

3. **Observe** How does water affect your skin? Record your observations.

_____

_____

Conclude and Apply

1. **Compare and Contrast** How does your skin feel when you touch it? When you blow on it? When you breathe on it?

_____

_____

2. Hypothesize How does water affect your skin? What does this
tell you about what skin can keep in or keep out of your body?

_____

_____

_____

Going Further: Apply

3. Draw Conclusions What do you think some of the jobs of the
skin are? How do you know?

_____

_____

_____

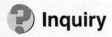 **Inquiry**

Think of your own questions about the skin that you might like to test.
What else can the skin feel?

My Question Is:

_____

_____

How I Can Test It:

_____

_____

My Results Are:

_____

_____

Skin Sense

Hypothesize How do different parts of your skin help you find out about the world around you?

Write a **Hypothesis:**

_____

Materials

• 3 or 4 classroom objects

Procedures

1. **Observe** Close your eyes. Have your partner place 3 or 4 objects on your desk. Roll up one of your sleeves and try to find out about the objects with your elbow. Record your observations.

_____

_____

_____

_____

2. **Observe** Now try to find out about the objects with your hand. Record your observations.

_____

_____

_____

_____

_____

Conclude and Apply

1. **Compare and Contrast** What did you find out about each object using your elbow? What did you find out about each object using your hand?

_____

_____

_____

2. **Draw Conclusions** Which part of your body made it easier to feel differences between the objects? Which part of your body made it harder? Why?

_____

_____

_____

Going Further Think about your own questions that you might like to test. What other information about the world around you can different parts of your skin help you find out?

My Question Is:

_____

_____

How I Can Test It:

_____

_____

My Results Are:

_____

_____

Investigate How the Body Protects Itself

Hypothesize Which parts of your body help protect you from invading germs? How might you use a model to test your ideas?

Write a **Hypothesis:**

_____

Use a model to investigate how your body protects itself from invading germs.

Materials

- sugar
- clay
- a comb
- 3 paper cups
- water
- a sheet of paper
- sticky tape

Procedures

1. **Make a Model** Write the words *EAR, SKIN, STOMACH, EYE,* and *NOSE* across a piece of paper. Press the clay above the word *EAR.* The clay stands for earwax. Draw bricks over the word *SKIN.* The bricks stand for dead cells in the epidermis. Wad up a piece of the sticky tape and drop the wad inside one of the cups. It stands for mucus. Place the cup above the word *NOSE* and lay the comb on top of the cup. The comb stands for nose hairs.

2. **Observe** The sugar stands for germs. Drop some sugar on the clay, comb, and bricks. What happens? Write your observations.

_____

_____

_____

3. **Make a Model** Turn a cup over and place it above the word *EYE.* Place a cup over the word *STOMACH.*

4. **Observe** Drop some sugar on the upside-down cup. Add a few drops of water. The water stands for tears. What happens? Drop some sugar into the cup that stands for the stomach. Add water. This time the water stands for stomach juices.

_____

_____

Conclude and Apply

1. **Infer** Name some ways the body protects itself from invading germs?

_____

_____

Going Further: Problem Solving

2. **Make a Model** What happens to germs when you have a cut in your skin? How might you use a model to find out?

_____

_____

Inquiry

Think of your own questions that you might like to test. How do germs enter your body?

My Question Is:

_____

How I Can Test It:

_____

My Results Are:

_____

Making a Model

Germs and Antibodies

A key must fit a lock or the lock won't open. Just like a key in a lock, an antibody has to fit a germ for the antibody to work correctly. You can make a model to show this. Making a model means constructing a representation of something. The model can be used to explain how something works.

Materials

• construction paper   • scissors

Procedures

1. Cut the construction paper into several squares. Then cut the squares into two pieces, like a puzzle. Label one half of each cutout with the letter G. The G stands for germ. Label the other part of the cutout with the letter A. The A stands for antibody.

2. **Make a Model** Swap your G and A pieces with pieces from another group. Try to match each G piece to an A piece. How many pairs fit together? Record the number. Return the G and A pieces to the group that made them.

   _____

3. Change some of your shapes. You might tear or fold a small section of the paper.

4. **Make a Model** Repeat step 2. How many pairs fit together now?

   _____

Conclude and Apply

1. **Compare and Contrast** What happened the first time you matched shapes together? What happened the second time? Record your results in the table.

	Number of Shapes that Matched
First Time	
Second Time	

Going Further: Apply

2. **Communicate** Use your model to explain why it is important for an antibody to fit a germ.

_____

_____

_____

_____

_____

Investigate What's in Food

Hypothesize How can you tell what is in different foods?

Write a **Hypothesis:**

_____

_____

Look for clues of whether these foods contain substances called fats.

Materials

• samples of different foods   • scissors   • brown paper bags

Procedures

1. Your teacher will give you samples of different foods. Predict which ones you think contain fat. Write your predictions.

_____

_____

2. **Experiment** Cut the paper bag into squares. Write the name of each food on a square. Rub a little of each food on the square that has its name. Let the squares dry for an hour.

3. **Observe** What has happened to the paper squares? Record your observations in the table below.

Food	Observations

Conclude and Apply

1. Identify Foods that contain a lot of fats often leave a greasy mark on surfaces they touch. Can you identify which of the foods contain fats?

_____

_____

2. Infer What can you say about the foods that left no greasy mark on the paper?

_____

Going Further: Apply

3. Classify Divide the foods into two groups. In one group place the foods that contain fats. In the second group place the foods that do not. What can you say about these two groups of foods?

_____

❓ Inquiry

Think of your own questions that you might like to test.
What other foods are low in fats?

My Question Is:

_____

How I Can Test It:

_____

_____

My Results Are:

_____

_____

Interpreting Data

Reading a Nutrition Label

Most foods have a nutrition label on them. A nutrition label lists the amounts of different nutrients in the food. The information in the label can help you identify which foods are good for you to eat. Look at the label pictured. Each line gives you information, or data. For example, look at the line labeled Serving Size. It says 1 container. This is the amount of food that is recommended you eat at one time. Now look at the line labeled Protein. How many grams of protein are there in one serving of this food? By answering this question, you are interpreting data. Interpret the data on the nutrition labels given to you to answer the questions below.

Materials

• food nutrition labels

Procedures

1. Look at the nutrition labels given to you. List the names of the foods in the table below.

2. **Interpret Data** Look at the food labels. How much fat is in one serving of each food? How much protein? Carbohydrates? Record the amount of each nutrient in the table.

Yogurt

Nutrition Facts
Serving Size   1 container   220 g

Amount per serving
Calories   195
Calories from Fat   27

% Daily value*

Total Fat	3 g	5%
Cholesterol	12 mg	6%
Sodium	155 mg	7%
Potassium	510 mg	15%
Total carbohydrate	33 g	12%
Fiber	0 g	0%
Sugars	32 g	
Protein	12 g	
Vitamin A	4%	
Vitamin C	4%	
Calcium	40%	
Iron	0%	

Ingredients: Grade A milk, skim milk, sugar, natural vanilla flavor, pectin, active yogurt cultures

* *Percent Daily Values are based on a 2,000 calorie diet.*

Food	Fat	Protein	Carbohydrates

3. Interpret Data What other nutrients are in each of the foods?
Are there vitamins and minerals? Does the food contain fiber?

_____

_____

_____

_____

_____

_____

_____

Conclude and Apply

1. **Compare and Contrast** Which food has the most fat? Which
   has the least? Which food has the most carbohydrates? Which
   has the least? Which has the most protein? Which has the least?

_____

_____

_____

2. **Evaluate** Which of these foods should you try to avoid?
   Which foods should you eat more often? Why?

_____

_____

_____

_____

_____

Investigate How Food Is Broken Down

Hypothesize How is food broken down? Remember that foods may be broken down in more than one way.

Write a **Hypothesis:**

_____

_____

Model how the body breaks down food.

Materials

- a small baked potato
- a paper towel
- a fork
- a piece of aluminum foil

Procedures

1. Place the paper towel on top of the foil. Place the potato on top of the paper towel.

2. **Experiment** How can you use the fork to divide the potato into smaller pieces? Record and test your ideas.

_____

_____

3. **Experiment** How can you use the fork to crush the potato into even smaller pieces?

_____

_____

4. **Observe** What happens if you squeeze the pieces of potato in the paper towel? Throw the towel and the pieces of potato in a wastebasket.

_____

Conclude and Apply

1. Compare and Contrast How did the potato change from the
beginning of the activity to the end?

_____

2. Communicate How were you able to break apart the potato?

_____

3. Infer What do you think came out
of the potato when you squeezed it? _____

Going Further: Apply

4. Infer Which part of your body do you think cuts and crushes food?
How do you know?

_____

_____

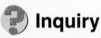 **Inquiry**

Think of your own questions that you might like to test. What foods
are easier to break down?

My Question Is:

_____

_____

How I Can Test It:

_____

_____

My Results Are:

_____

Eating a Cracker

Hypothesize Does digestion begin in the mouth?

Write a **Hypothesis:**

_____

_____

Materials

• 1 unsalted cracker

Procedures

Observe Slowly chew the cracker for 1 minute. Observe all the ways the cracker changes inside your mouth. Swallow the cracker.

Conclude and Apply

1. **Identify** How did the shape of the cracker change inside your mouth?

_____

_____

2. **Compare and Contrast** How did the cracker taste when you put it in your mouth? How did it taste right before you swallowed it?

_____

_____

_____

3. Draw Conclusions Does digestion begin in the mouth? How do you know?

_____

_____

Going Further Think of your own questions that you might like to test. How do other foods change in your mouth?

My Question Is:

_____

How I Can Test It:

_____

My Results Are:

_____

_____